Escape From 1984

Subtitle: There's Something Very Fishy Going on, it's
More Than Just a Virus!

By Chris Briscoe ©

Published by Chris Briscoe Publishers©

August 15th, 2021.

INTRODUCTION:

IT'S NOT ABOUT A VIRUS, IT'S ABOUT RESETTING THE ENTIRE ECONOMY.

"Meyer Amschel Rothschild, who founded the great international banking house of Rothschild which, through its affiliation with the European Central Banks, still dominates the financial policies of practically every country in the world, said: 'Permit me to issue and control the money of a nation, and I care not who makes its laws.' "
Mayer Amschel Rothschild

"For the first time in its history, Western Civilization is in danger of being destroyed internally by a corrupt, criminal ruling cabal which is centered around the Rockefeller interests, which include elements from the

Morgan, Brown, Rothschild, Du Pont, Harriman, Kuhn-Loeb, and other groupings as well. This junta took control of the political, financial, and cultural life of America in the first two decades of the twentieth century."
Carroll Quigley

"The issuing power [of money] should be taken from the banks and restored to the people, to whom it properly belongs."
Thomas Jefferson

"I believe that banking institutions are more dangerous to our liberties than standing armies."
Thomas Jefferson

"For the last one hundred and fifty years, the history of the House of Rothschild has been to an amazing

degree the backstage history of Western Europe...Because of their success in making loans not to individuals but to nations, they reaped huge profits...Someone once said that the wealth of Rothschild consists of the bankruptcy of nations."
Frederic Morton

"If you want to know who holds the real power in nations, it's not the one who holds the gavel in the legislator but rather who holds the national purse strings – the one who issues the money, which, in the case of the U.K. is the Bank of England.

If you think that this is about a virus, then I believe you have been conned, because I believe it's about the resetting of the economy and about the Government having more control over what you do, where you go and what you can buy or sell, in the name of your health. "
Chris Briscoe.

"When the State reverts to the instruments of coercion, i.e. propaganda, fear, and even the threat of sending in the army on the streets, as well as the threat of fines and imprisonment when at the time, such coercions are no way justified, then it means the Government has become tyrannical; instruments of the State which Boris used unjustly since they were used disproportionately when weighing the risks of this virus carrying a 99.98% survival rate to the under 40s and a 99.99% survival rate to the under 20s, i.e. it was like using a sledge hammer to approach a pea."
Chris Briscoe.

CHAPTER ONE.

Here Follows the Memoir of Master Joe Bloggs.

My name is Joe Bloggs from the U.K.; now a highschool senior in public school, i.e. one of your government run and financed schools. I will use the American-usage of middleschool and highschool instead of the more simple, secondary school for the reason that, although that term "secondary school" is succinct, it does not differentiate between middle and high except if you were to say "upper" or "lower", so for the sake of our friends, "over the Pond" I will use their Americanism of middle school and high school, and junior and senior.

My dear parents named me, Joe Bloggs because they

wanted me to be someone of convention and stability but I don't think I am your typical Joe Bloggs.

When I was in middle school, my teacher told me to read the dystopian book "1984" by George Orwell. She said it was required reading. No one ever warned me that the U.K. could end up as a near dystopian country by the year 2024, much like the much diminished Great Britain in that book, whose new name became "Airstrip One" after the forces of Marxism had had their way – whether it was Marxism or another form of socialism or communism , one things for sure, whenever violence is involved to implement tyranny, it's a form of fascism.

And that's why that organization in the U.S. is crying out to be banned as a terrorist or violent organization called "Antifa" because it's regularly terrorizing its own people with raw violence which you can see on You Tube or Twitter; that word is supposed to mean anti-facism, but if you think about it, that word, "anti-fa" i.e. anti-fascism is being misused because it's a misnomer, i.e. a misnamed name because it, itself, is a fascist organisation since it uses violence. What defines fascism and a person as fascist isn't your political ideology but rather your use of violence.

That's why, even though Adolf Hitler was actually a socialist, i.e. from the left politically while Benito Mussolini was from the far right politically, they used the same tactics of dealing with the opposition through violence and intimidation. Even though Hitler and Mussolini were at opposite ends of the political spectrum, they were both violent, and maybe that's why they were such close allies, in fact, friends throughout the Second World War, and before.

As for my own country, the U.K. Government are not violent in dealing with those who challenge them, themselves, but they have plenty of other instruments of tyranny to use, and even though they may not use violence, they are using a form of violence, I call "soft violence" when they violate you and I – our bodies and minds through the more subtler weapons of tyranny, i.e. propaganda, through fear and through the threat of fines and imprisonment, and the sanctioning of our freedoms to introduce their undemocratic new policies of lockdowns, vaccination passports which violate our personal consent to what goes into our bodies by mandating that we are no longer free to use our freedoms anymore. Whether that is because they, themselves, want to follow the Globalists agenda of infiltrating our bodies through what's called, "the Internet of Bodies". I mean, whether it is because Boris Johnson feels threatened enough to be in the pockets of the Globalist or Banksters, one thing is certain, he is compromised either by fear or tyranny, or probably both, and because he is controlled by fear, the entire country is controlled by fear. But I will tell you later what I found out.

This nation of what was once called Great Britain among the throngs has become almost "Little Britain", with its leaders and people cowering in fear. That's why fear is the most potent force in persuading a people, along with propaganda and threats of fines or imprisonment, and even the army on the streets, which Boris Johnson has threatened his own people repeatedly, using also the tyranny and even violence of British police forces in banning every Joe and Josephine Blogs from their right to demonstrate on the streets and lobby the government and the Establishment for justice and change, because in the name of our health, they told us that more than one person couldn't gather.

Boris has allowed this once, good but not perfect

country of the United Kingdom with its Christian faith, to be taken over and controlled by fear, FEAR - which is the antithetical to the Christian power and virtue of love.

When the nation of the U.S.A. or its people were spiraling out of control from fear of ruin, after the 1929 financial crash, what did President Franklin Delano Roosevelt say in his first of what would be three Inaugural Ceremonies:

"So, first of all, let me assert my firm belief that the only thing we have to fear is, fear itself — nameless, unreasoning, unjustified terror which paralyzes needed efforts to convert retreat into advance. In every dark hour of our national life, a leadership of frankness and of vigour has met with that understanding and support of the people themselves which is essential to victory. And I am convinced that you will again give that support to leadership in these critical days."

Fear and propaganda are the instruments of tyranny. For example, throughout this "Covid-19 pandemic " when the Prime Minister, Boris Johnson, stands before the nation, and the two doctors or professors who flank him, Messrs. Chris Whitty and Patrick Vallance, if you are awake, they all use data models, not actual data "to put the fear of hell into you", which are politically biased, i.e. the numbers they use are worse-case scenarios to make you think, that unless we lockdown the nation, there will be thousands that die of Covid-19. Indeed, when the United Kingdom and the U.S.A. first locked-down or closed their economies, it was because their leaders had been shown computer models published by the Imperial College of London, and written by Professor Neil Ferguson when he predicted that,unless we lockdown, 510,000 people would die of Covid-19.

We have learned from Neil Ferguson's 's interview in
"The Times Newspaper" that the U.K. Government and
its team of advisors at SAGE didn't think that they
could introduce and implement lockdowns in a
democratic country until Italy had done it in the name
of controlling their epidemic.

As Professor Ferguson revealed in a recent interview
with The Times:

"I think people's sense of what is possible in terms of
control changed quite dramatically between January
and March," Professor Ferguson says. When SAGE
observed the "innovative intervention" out of China, of
locking entire communities down and not permitting
them to leave their homes, they initially presumed it
would not be an available option in a liberal Western
democracy:

"It's a communist one party state, we said. We couldn't get away with it in Europe, we thought… and then Italy did it. And we realised we could."

"These days, lockdown feels inevitable. It was, he reminds me, anything but. "If China had not done it," he says, "the year would have been very different.""

- PROFESSOR NEIL FERGUSON, IMPERIAL COLLEGE,

THE TIMES NEWSPAPER.

The Times reporter writes, "To those people who, still now, object to lockdowns on civil liberties principles, this will be a chilling reminder of the centrality of the authoritarian Chinese model in influencing global policy in this historic year.

"That's China. But then Italy locked down and suddenly we thought, well, if Italy, a democratic nation in Europe, can do it, can get away with it, so can we."

At least, that's what Professor Neil Ferguson - whose nickname is "Professor Lockdown" among some - was recommending the U.K. and the U.S. Government do when they both went into Lockdown in March 2020 through his papers published by Imperial College. Neil Ferguson's was using code for his computer modelling to predict 510,000 deaths if we didn't lockdown the country. In the interview to the Times, he maintains that because Britain went into lockdown, we were not facing such a large loss of life. However, if you ask any other epidemiologist, they would agree that a figure of 510,000 is way, way off the mark.

This was not the only time he has been proved wrong, indeed, if you Look at his Record of Over-Predictions, it is a wonder that the U.K.Government keep Inquiring his "expertise":

Imperial College epidemiologist, Neil Ferguson was behind the disputed research that sparked the mass culling of eleven million sheep and cattle during the 2001 outbreak of foot-and-mouth disease. He also predicted that up to 150,000 people could die. There were fewer than 200 deaths.

Also, In 2002, Professor Ferguson predicted that up to 50,000 people would likely die from exposure to BSE (mad cow disease) in beef. In the U.K., there were only 177 deaths from BSE.

Also, in 2005, Profesor Ferguson predicted that up to 150 million people could be killed from bird flu. In the end, only 282 people died worldwide from the disease between 2003 and 2009.

And then, In 2009, a government estimate, based on Ferguson's advice, said a "reasonable worst-case scenario" was that the swine flu would lead to 65,000 British deaths. In the end, swine flu killed 457 people in the U.K.

Last March, Professor Ferguson admitted that his Imperial College model of the COVID-19 disease was based on undocumented, 13-year-old computer code that was intended to be used for a feared influenza pandemic, rather than a coronavirus. Ferguson declined to release his original code so other scientists could check his results. He only released a heavily revised set of code last week, after a six-week delay.

Thus the real scandal is why does the U.K. Government keep using him and his future predictions, when they have all proved totally wrong, not just wrong but apocalyptically wrong, predicting apocalyptic scenarios if we don't cull millions of cattle or lockdown the country.

Why did anyone ever listen to this guy?

Maybe, Professor Ferguson is becoming mellow in his predictions. As the report from, "Breitbart" reported, in their 8th August Article, Link https://www.breitbart.com/europe/2021/08/08/professor-lockdown-admits-doomsday-predictions-were-off/

"Professor Lockdown" Dr Neil Ferguson has admitted that his latest doomsday predictions about a summer wave of the Chinese virus were "off" and has now revised his thinking to predict that the pandemic will largely be over by the Autumn, transforming into a virus that the public will have to "live with". Professor Ferguson, an epidemiologist from Imperial College London and advisor to the government during the Chinese coronavirus crisis, predicted on Saturday that the era of lockdowns is likely over in Britain.

As for those other two professors on Boris left and right during his frequent Covid-19 announcements, I feel forced to give them alternative nicknames of "Dr. Doom" and "Dr. Gloom" because that's all the news they give - even last Autumn, Dr. Gloom said that he thinks that the U.K. should have a lockdown every winter and this one shouldn't end until the end of Autumn; of which this Government, cannot give a date, neither a projected date nor even a month, let alone a season when this third Lockdown of Devastation will be lifted.

And so if you want a clue as to what is really driving this global "pandemic", crisis or rather "plandemic" of fear well, look to what has in the past usually governed and controlled and driven each nation's agenda and policy, which is money, or rather the love of money, i.e. greed, or the other just as potent force the fear of not having enough money, so the best way, if I was a detective, I would always follow the money trail, or follow what the Chinese Communist Party is implementing, and also follow the motive of the Cabal

of Banksters , i.e. those who control the money supply or control the power of spending finances and lending financing as well as debt -
the BIG BANKS AS WELL AS THOSE WHO HAVE A LOT OF MONEY OR ARE COMING INTO BIG MONEY WITH THESE VACCINES, THE BIG PHARMA.

And I believe Boris is following the way of the Globalists following the example of the Chinese Communist Party who know every citizen mind or intention or political nuance through their digital tattoo, who want a complete cashless society where everyone becomes just a number with a code of allegiance where everyone is categorized into State Compliant or Adversant.

When the State reverts to the instruments of propaganda, fear, coercion, and even the threat of sending in the army on the streets, as well as the threat of fines and imprisonment when at the time, such coercions in no way are justified, then it means the Government has become tyrannical; instruments of the State which Boris used unjustly since they were used disproportionately when weighing the risks of this virus carried a 99.98 survival rate to the under 40 and 99.99% survival rate to the under 20, i.e. it was like using a sledge hammer to approach a pea.

And when this Covid-19 first started or erupted onto our screens, why is it that the under 40 have a 99.98 % survival rate, and that increases to 99.99 for the under 20's survival rate for this disease. When in the space of 15 months those who died in England and Wales amounted to just 25 under twenty-five.

Is it any wonder why I feel the State is using three main instruments of tyranny, propaganda, i.e.

Government lies, fear, and modes of more direct coercion such as fines, imprisonment, and threats of the army being sent onto the streets, which Boris Johnson has made on at least one occasion.

But why is this? Do they have another agenda and that's why they favour lockdowns? And what's happened to Boris Johnson, who used to be a self-proclaimed libertine, who before, he himself, was struck with a bad bout of Covid-19 which almost killed him, he seemed to follow that libertine spirit and bolt at the idea of lockdowns, indeed his own ex-advisor testified that Boris was reluctant, at first, to place the U.K. into lockdown; when he finally placed the country into lockdown, it was a full month after France and the other major European nations.

But Look at What is Happening in the U.K. after Three Lockdowns.

No one ever warned me that the scenario of "1984" could come to my own country, the U.K, by 2024, no one except George Orwell.

George Orwell wrote the following :

"In a time of deceit telling the truth is a revolutionary act."

"Who controls the past,' ran the Party slogan, 'controls the future: who controls the present controls the past.'"

"The most effective way to destroy people is to deny and obliterate their own understanding of their history."

That's the real reason these Marxist forces or fascist forces are violently tearing down our statues of past figures, of the great, the good, and the nit so good. Because they want to erase our history when they deem it unsavoury in their eyes, because he who controls the past, controls the present and the future.

SOMETHING IS NOT RIGHT WITH THIS COVID-19 PANDEMIC.

I am only sixteen years old, yet I can see when I use my brain that something is not right about this so-called Covid-19 pandemic. SOMETHING LOOKS VERY FISHY TO ME. And I'm not talking about the disease, I am talking about the response to this disease, i.e. the way our politicians, i.e. leaders have responded to this disease, which some politicians have responded well, e.g. the Governor of Florida, Ronald DeSantis who responded proportionately to the risk, while other leaders, for example, my nation's leader, Boris Johnson, who responded like holding a mallet to crack open a garden-pea, and as well as obliterating that pea, he has destroyed millions and millions of businesses and livelihoods from his three lockdowns when he shut down the nation for a disease which, if you are over 50, you have a 99.97 % survival rate if you catch it, which rises to 99.98 % if you are under 50.

If you Look at the following image, you will see that actually this Covid-19 is part of a family of diseases which include the common colds. I got these facts and the image from a Doctor Keith Moran, a Medical Doctor in Gastroenterology, Cardiology, and Echocardiography, who you can find on the Internet broadcasting on You Tube Videos, which you can watch, at least now, before his channel is taken down for its "unorthodoxy" with "We are following the science" community.

Human Coronaviruses

• Common Cold Coronaviruses:
   HCoV-229E, HCoV-NL63, HCoV-OC43, HCoV-HKU1

• Severe coronavirus infections:
   SARS-CoV, SARS-CoV-2, and MERS-CoV

Medicine with Dr. Mor

fatalities have been people 65 and older.
https://www.bloomberg.com/opinion/articles/
2021-03-01/covid-19-s-death-toll-compared-to-other-
things-that-kill-us

"There's nothing unusual about this age profile — in fact, the different age groups' share of Covid deaths is strikingly similar to their share of deaths, period."

THIS IS WHAT I HAVE LEARNED DOING MY OWN RESEARCH:

This, Covid-19 is actually a disease which strikes the old rather than the young, although there are, of course exceptions, so unless your child has underlying health problems, i.e. a compromised immune system, the risks from the Covid-19 vaccinations are higher than the risks from the actual disease Covid-19.

Now if you look at the next image, it shows you the percentage of people dying from this disease. i.e. the fatality rate of the different diseases so you can compare:

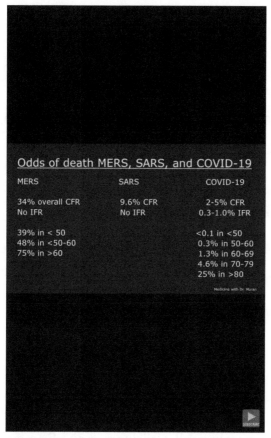

The information this Dr. Keith Moran gives out in these diseases seems reliable, since the numbers or fatality rate he uses are a cross average which means he doesn't just rely on one study or one data, but a number of studies and data to get an average which is more reliable.

So as a sixteen year old, I have some questions to Boris Johnson,

Why did you shut down the country three times during this Covid-era for a virus which kills 3 people every one thousand people or 0.3 percent of the population if you are aged between 50-60?

It seems to a sixteen year old a rather disproportionate response, of stopping all children including me, from getting on with our education for at least a year, and stopping everyone getting on with our lives for sixteen months for a virus which kills less than 0.3 of the population, i.e. 3 persons in every one thousand of the population if you are aged 50-60? And which lowers to

0.2 of the population or two persons in every thousand people of the population for those aged below fifty years.

Which means as the above figures shows in the image, if you are aged between 50-60 you have a 99.97% chance of surviving the Covid-19 which rises to 99.98 % chance of survival if you are under fifty. And of course, that figure lowers even more with those under forty and thirty years old, and twenty years, and ten years. And even if you consider the new Covid-19 variants in these figures, which are supposedly hitting a higher rate of younger people compared with the original Covid-19, we can still say that if you are over fifty, you still have a 0.1 % or one in a thousand fatality rate.

Yes, admittedly, the virus is risky for people aged between 60-69 which kills 1.3 persons every one hundred persons; or 4.6 persons every one hundred for people aged 70-79, and a whopping 25 in every one hundred for over 80 years olds.

So, instead of quarantining the healthy for almost fifteen months for a virus which kills less than one person every one hundred persons, why didn't you just quarantine the sick, aged and vulnerable like in previous pandemics?

Not once, in the history of pandemics – including bubonic plague which killed a third of Europe's population, have we quarantined healthy people, but only the sick. But for this disease, with its roughly 99.97% survival rate, Boris quarantined us three times. And the people complied.

In the U.S., Eighty-one percent of U.S. Covid-19

During my research, I found out that this Covid-19 disease whose actual proper name is SARS-Covi-2 is actually SARS-2 following from SARS-Covi (i.e.SARS-Covi-1) which was a previous outbreak that occurred in 2003 which you can call SARS-1 while this Covid-19 is SARS-2.

If you look again at the above images, can you also see that other Covid outbreak, which originated from mainly Saudi Arabia in the Middle East, so called Middle Eastern Respiratory Syndrome, i.e. MERS, of which the name of the disease is MERS-CoV which was a disease transmitted to humans from camels, although the reservoir, meaning the original host that is not affected by its own disease, was most likely bats? Again, if you look at his image, under MERS disease it has a death rate, i.e. fatality rate of 34% or 35% but this could be an overestimate because it doesn't take into account possible milder, unreported cases; yet you can see how much more infectious and deadlier is was: under Covid-19 it has a death rate of 0.03% for under 50s rising to 0.02% for under 40s.

If you look at the SARS-1 i.e.SARS-Covi-1 which also originated from China, which affected 29 countries, it had a 10 % death rate which was huge compared to SARS-2, i.e. SARS-Covi-2, i.e. Covid-19 Starting in 2002, this epidemic lasted about one and a half years, infecting at least 8,000 people and killing 10% of them. Although it mostly affected east Asian countries, by its end SARS-1 had spread worldwide

BUT DID TONY BLAIR, THE BRITISH PRIME MINISTER, LOCK DOWN THE NATION OF THE U.K. WHEN SARS 1 BECAME A WORLD PANDEMIC?

NO.

SO WHILE A DISEASE, i.e. SARS 1, RAVAGED TEN PERCENT OF THE POPULATION IN 2003, BUT PRIME MINISTER BLAIR DIDN'T LOCKDOWN, WHY DID BORIS SHUT DOWN THE U.K. THREE TIMES WITH A DISEASE, i.e. Covid-19 HITTING LESS THAN 1 PERCENT OF THE POPULATION?

My parents, who are old enough to remember about that SARS 1 Pandemic that struck mostly East Asia, they remember China and Hong Kong being placed in lockdown, when both the healthy and the sick were not allowed to go out or mix with other people. None of the other nations of the world went into lockdown, as far as I know, although compared with SARS-2 (Covid-19), only 28,096 people got SARS-1 and 774 of them died.

Also, if you take the disease Ebola which isn't included in the image, that had a rate infecting over 40% of the population, a disease which originated from the River Ebola in 1976, in Africa, and which has affected a total of nine countries, including one aid worker in the U.K. returning from Africa, yet the British Government didn't lockdown the nation, although Ebola was never transmitted to another British Nation in the U.K.

And if, as Boris claimed, when he first announced a lockdown on the 21st March, 2020, "We are following the science", and if his motive for these lockdowns is the public's health and wellbeing then what about the pandemic of fear, the pandemic of depression and mental sickness these lockdowns are causing all for a disease which kills less than 3 in a thousand?

And if lockdowns were so effective at controlling this virus, with the U.K. having had three prolonged lockdowns, how come the U.K. has had the worst record in Europe of nearly 120,000 deaths as of March, 2021, from Covid-19 when other nations such as Sweden which never locked-down, has of the 23rd

March, a record of 13,120 deaths for the same period?

If we compare those countries that did lockdown compared with those nations that didn't; for example, Sweden, between March, 10th, 2020, to March, 2021,the number of recorded deaths are 3,111 people. Yet, in the same period for the U.K. which have been locked-down for almost a year, there have been at least 120,000 deaths. So the question is well overdue to be asked why are we having these lockdowns if the evidence shows they don't work, even if we take into consideration that the two nations are very different in that the U.K. is much more busier in regard to visitors, however, the fact that Boris ten months and eleven days to finally close down the borders. We need to ask these questions, but who's asking these questions? Did Sweden close its borders during this period?

The first lockdown lasted seven weeks, after Boris and

his advisors initially saying it would probably be three weeks to flatten the curve, and then, after the summer months, in November there was a new lockdown. This new lockdown started in England on January 5 at one minute past midnight. Therefore, throughout this year, the 'stay at home' order was enforced which means that everyone has to stay inside wherever possible and only leave their home for essential reasons. Strictly speaking, while the 'stay at home' order was lifted, England and the rest of the UK never fully left lockdown like other countries such as New Zealand have. In autumn 2020, the first three tier system was announced before being replaced with a month's worth of lockdown in November. If we had followed New Zealand's example, I believe comparing the U.K with New Zealand is good because its also an island nation or a nation of Islands.

After the second lockdown, England was once again placed in a new and revised tier system with many areas immediately going into the highest tier of almost lockdown. This means that the country had been operating in a form of lockdown for over 10 months now. And then a few days before Christmas the Government announced Tier Five, complete lockdown, for all of London and parts of the South East only after three days before, the Prime Minister stood up in Parliament and said that cancelling Christmas would be inhuman. So, except for a few exceptions like being let out once a day for exercise or for food or only allowed out if we can't work at home and a list of other exceptions, the U.K. population feel like they are living in a giant prison all-be-it under house arrest.

These are questions that me, a teenager, wants to ask Boris Johnson because I noticed, nobody else is asking such questions. Not the Labour Party who is Her Majesty's Opposition, who are paid handsomely for that honour, of which their official name is, "Her Majesty's Most Loyal Opposition", or "the Official

Opposition", in the United Kingdom, is the main political opposition to Her Majesty's Government. Yet, they are not holding the current Government to account as is their job, nor is the so called Mainstream Media who have now become the Lamestream Media, because they are also, not doing their job.

Now, if I had told you back in January, 2020, that within the space of 18 months a mysterious, invisible disease known as Covid-19 with a fatality survival rate of 99.97 % would result in Boris Johnson's Government introducing Covid-19 Vaccine-Status Passports into British society which you had to show at the entrance of nightclubs or venues of at least two hundred people, and that everyone outside their homes in South Korea would be forced to wear a mask - not just on public transport but everywhere they roam - you might have thought I had been reading too many sci-fi books. And if I was to say the police would be arresting people for merely sitting down on a park bench in England, you might have told me that this is Britain not North Korea.

In George Orwell's book 1984, the weapons the State uses are the same propaganda as North Korea and China, i.e. propaganda, which is another word for State lies; they have other weapons, such as fear and coercion with the threat of fines or imprisonment. Now the U.K.can be added to that list of North Korea, China as nations of State using tyranny. North Korea also employs public executions as another instrument of tyranny.

In that book, "1984", the telescreen was the device "Big Brother" - the State - used to spy on you, but today our Smart-phones are what the state uses to spy on you, meaning we are almost all carrying our own personal telescreen in our pockets in which we are being spied on by Facebook, Google etc, by Silicon

Valley in California, through our online activity. However, for certain organizations or people, these peeks into our lives are not enough, and not obtrusive enough to obtain a deep enough view of our lives as they do not have the potential to control us, only observe us from a distance.

But, when I did more research on this matter, I found out that there is a plan being undertaken which is trying to get, not just into our lives but into our very bodies, called "The Internet of Bodies", which certain people, and organisations, including the World Economic Forum is taking advantage of this Covid-19 crisis to bring in their agenda of resetting the entire world economy and introducing thus Internet of Bodies so their vision of the future where no one owns anything but everyone will be happy, where the world is owned and everyone is owned by a small group of rich Elitists, but, in their estimate, you will be happy because, like the black African slaves in past centuries who owned nothing, they were free of debt because they were owned by somebody.

Do you remember the time when we Britons could go overseas when we wanted, could go outside for a walk when we wanted, even could hug our grandmother who because she was outside our "bubble" hugging grandmother was banned by the Government?

In the space of 15 months, the people of the U.K. have been through three lockdowns, which meant apart from the few intermediate months when each region was placed in either a red, orange or yellow colour system of a three-tiered-system, and then at Christmas a further fourth teir, the British people were asked to stay at home, effectively in almost house-arrest for sixteen months, unless they couldn't work from home; the rules were we were only allowed out of their house once for exercise or to buy essentials.

As for myself, who spent almost one year at home, educated by myself, or by my parents when they were home, coming through the last almost two years of what people are calling the Covid era or Covid times, and experiencing all that has transpired, I am a lot wiser for it.

I mean I have learned some great lessons. Now I am in my highschool years, actually, the final year of highschool before I try for a place at University; and having been through these past two years of Covid-19 in 2020-2021, I have wised-up after learning some powerful lessons. For example, I have learned the following, and I write in capitals in my memoir to remind me:

NEVER, I REPEAT ONE HUNDRED TIMES, NEVER TRUST THE GOVERNMENT ON ANYTHING THEY

SAY, OR ANYTHING THEY TELL YOU TO DO BECAUSE THEY DON'T ALWAYS HAVE YOUR BEST INTERESTS AT HEART.

AND IF THERE'S ONE THING WE LEARNED IN THE PAST 18 MONTHS OF THIS COVID ERA, NEVER TRUST ANY OFFICIAL DATA, AND DEFINITELY NOT ANY GOVERNMENT ADVISORS WHO SHOW YOU THEIR MODELING BECAUSE EVERY MODELING WHICH DOCTORS PATRICK VALLANCE, AND CHRIS WHITTY AND NEIL FERGUSON HAVE USED TO JUSTIFY A LOCKDOWN, HAVEN'T JUST BEEN WRONG BUT THOUSANDS OF TIMES, WRONG.

Because their data and decisions are based on modelling which relies on conjecture, meaning they make predictions, yet predicting a scenario couldn't be more political because the scenario you predict depends on your political bias including who you work for; or in the case of Messrs Vallance, Whitty, and Ferguson, as they work for Boris Johnson, and Boris prefers lockdowns, they always present a worse-case scenario of data projecting thousands of deaths a day, and cases, which have always proved wrong, later, when the damage has been done, more by their lockdowns than anything else. To be fair Neil Ferguson is apparently an unpaid worker but I don't know how true that is.

When Boris first plunged the nation into a lockdown, unprecedented in its history, his reasons to shut down the country and tell people to stay at home was "to flatten the curve" and of course, they were given computer modelling from Neil Ferguson which predicted 510,000 people would lose their lives if we didn't lock down. But what they didn't tell us was that the peak of deaths had already been reached ten days before, and if you care to look at the actual data not computer models you will notice that the peak had already been reached when Boris was telling the nation to shut down.

Boris again locked-down the nation a second a time in November 2020, when the justification for lockdown was again based on models projecting the number of deaths this time 4000, not real data; Patrick Vallance told the nation that he predicted the scenario of 4000 deaths a day by the middle of November if we didn't lockdown. He stressed at the time, that the figure of 4000 was not data but a prediction of a worse-case scenario.

However, within a few minutes or hours after their Covid news announcements and the nation had gone into a second lockdown, that figure of 4,000 was proved false. Professor Carl Heneghan, director of the Centre for Evidence-Based Medicine at Oxford

University, urged Professor Chris Whitty and Sir Patrick Vallance to provide "really clear" information to MPs to explain why a second lockdown has been ordered when they appear in front of the Science and Technology Committee this afternoon.

As Dr. Heneghan said, the decision to impose new blanket restrictions must be made on "actual data" and not models that are "shown to be wrong", adding the Government's three-tier system was effective in bringing down coronavirus cases.

Professor Chris Whitty and Sir Patrick Vallance have been urged to give "really clear" information to MPs about why a second lockdown is needed. Data presented by the Government's chief advisers to justify a second national lockdown in England has been "mathematically proven" to be incorrect, an Oxford University professor has said.

Carl Heneghan, director of the Centre for Evidence-Based Medicine at the University of Oxford, said a forecast suggesting 4,000 daily deaths next month was wrong.

The modelling, which was presented at a Downing Street press conference on Saturday is so outdated that it suggests daily deaths are now around 1,000 a day.

In fact, the daily average for the last week is 260, with a figure of 162 on the Saturday.

But the 4,000 figure was presented by scientists when Boris Johnson confirmed new nationwide restrictions would be imposed from Thursday for four weeks to prevent a "medical and moral disaster" for the NHS.

Prof Heneghan told the Today programme: "Mathematically it is now proven to be incorrect particularly the 4,000 estimate of deaths that would occur in December and why that is because it is already about four weeks out of date.

"And actually Cambridge who are doing it the MRC (Medical Research Council) unit have already provided updates to provide lower estimates and those estimates are much closer to the truth."

Prof Heneghan urged Professor Chris Whitty and Sir Patrick Vallance to provide "really clear" information to MPs to explain why a second lockdown has been ordered when they appear in front of the Science and Technology Committee this afternoon.

He said the decision to impose new blanket restrictions

must be made on "actual data" and not models that are "shown to be wrong", adding the Government's three-tier system was effective in bringing down coronavirus cases.

Speaking about Liverpool, where the strictest restrictions have been imposed, Prof Heneghan said cases had halved while hospital admissions had "stabilised".

And when the number of deaths in the actual data were no longer enough to justify lockdowns, the Government S.A.G.E. group, i.e. the Science Advisory Group for Emergencies changed the way Covid figures were calculated. Did you notice that the SAGE Group changed from reporting deaths to reporting cases when they didn't have enough death cases. From that time, they started publishing cases of Covid cases rather than deaths because the number of deaths no longer justified more lockdowns. Even when cases including testing positive for COVID-19 which didn't mean they were actual individuals who had disease of Covid-19 because you could still test positive and yet be asymptomatic. This also inflated the figures further.

So What is the Real Reason for Shutting Down the Country Three Times, Boris?

So Boris Johnson, in shutting down the country, it actually looks to me like you have a different reason for causing disruption to an entire nation of 66.65 million people and devastation of our schools and economy because your cure does more damage than what this Covid-19 would have ever done. I mean, even if we had let this disease just have its way, while – like Sweden or Florida - we exercised good, common sense and social distancing, still the vast majority of the nation has a strong enough immunity or anti-bodies for this Covid-19 not to produce a huge problem - I mean nationally. Yes, of course, this disease is a deadly disease and I am not, for one second, trivialising the impact and suffering of numerous families who have suffered the loss of a loved-one, but as a nation, this Covid-19 does not present a risk enough to shut the entire nation down along with most businesses, with the hospitality industry - mostly hotel, restaurant, and pubs and bars - as well as the aviation industry having suffered the most; devastating millions of people's livelihoods and almost destroying our economy, with devastating consequences for us all, including record job losses, record mental-health issues, record marriage-breakdowns, record domestic violence and suicides.

So it makes me think that,
SOMETHING ELSE IS GOING ON,
THAT IT'S NOT ACTUALLY ABOUT A VIRUS BUT
RATHER ANOTHER REASON WHICH SOME

OPPORTUNISTS ARE TAKING ADVANTAGE OF FOR THEIR OWN SECRET AGENDA,

Which Boris, for some reason, either, he has bought into their agenda, i.e. believes their agenda - or worse, he has been coerced or threatened into following their agenda, or even more worse, he is following an agenda which is damaging the people of the U.K. and is actually an enemy of the U.K. in which case he has become a traitor to his own country.

Why is it that across the U.K, during a lockdown, the small shops, e.g. the small stationery shop selling greetings cards was told to shut down to contain the spread of Covid-19, while at the same time, the big stationery stores, e.g. W.H. Smith down the road, was allowed to keep opening selling stationary items and greetings cards during the Lockdown?

Is it because the agenda of the Globalists cabal around the world whose agenda is called "The Great Reset", which is the slogan of the World Economic Forum, are the same as the ones using the slogan, "Build Back Better" including the one that Boris has frequented in the past, the World Economic Forum, and which has the same slogan, "The Great Reset" and that Boris Johnson and Joe Biden have both used that slogan, "Build Back Better" for their own political slogans? A slogan that Boris uses frequently, even at the G7.

And this and the other slogan of "The Great Reset".

But What does that Great Reset mean?
Well, first of all, if you research about it, it is not great.

But What is the Relationship with this Covid-19 Pandemic?
This Covid-19 has an infection or transmission rate of

at least 50% of the population but its death-rate is between 0.5 and 0.75. Scientists have found that at least 60% of the population have had the disease in the past or have it now - or are asymptomatic - meaning they have the virus without symptoms. 84.5 percent of deaths attributed to the virus were of people aged 60 or older, according to the state's health department.

So, it looks very much like Boris Johnson and his advisors have been taken captive by fear and the entire country is following them, and the real virus is the virus of mistrust and the daily skewed data from our screens trying to inject us with more fear, complicity and compliance. And what you call a conspiracy theory is much, much nearer the truth than any other theories that have been offered. I tend to place great credence on her implication that this isn't about a virus but about the State and banks trying to reset the economy. If you look at history, even the history of most crises, the Governments of the West have never failed to miss taking advantage of a good crisis. Wait and see if her prediction of an October financial crash comes true before you condemn her.

What Has Happened To Boris?

We Expected so much Better from a Leader whose Hero is Winston Churchill, who liked him so much wrote a book about him.

And we have witnessed that the real damager or troubler or real deadlier variant is a variant of the old Boris Johnson,

I don't know what has happened to the old Boris. The old Boris before he was infected and almost died of Covid-19 would have said,

"HEY, PEOPLE, WE CAN FIGHT THIS, WE CAN OVERCOME, WE CAN WIN, IF WE JUST HAVE

SOME FAITH IN OURSELVES AND OUR STRONG IMMUNITY SYSTEM, WE CAN EASILY LICK THIS! THIS VIRUS IS ACTUALLY NOT THAT POWERFUL AND TOGETHER WE HAVE MORE THAN STRONG ENOUGH STRONG IMMUNE SYSTEM AND STRONG HEALTHY, YOUNG PEOPLE AMONGST US WHO WE CAN TOGETHER PRODUCE HERD IMMUNITY AND DRIVE THIS INVADER INTO THE SEA THE WAY WE DROVE ADOLF HITLER AND HIS VARIANTS INTO THE SEA. WE ARE SMART ENOUGH AND WISE ENOUGH TO PRACTICE GOOD SOCIAL DISTANCING FOR A WHILE, TO OVERCOME THIS - MOST OF US - MORE THAN 99.9999999% OF THE POPULATION HAVE A STRONG ENOUGH IMMUNE SYSTEM TO CAUSE THIS VIRUS TO BE ON THE RETREAT."

If Boris had said that, a policy similar to the policy implemented in Sweden and in the American state of Florida, then Boris would have been respected and admired in the same standing of his hero, Winston Churchill. And consequently, we would be facing a much better, more emboldened and empowered and stronger, more confident Britain than we are facing now. But now, after subjecting the nation to three lockdowns and even scandalously employing means of mind and psychological control over his own people to terrorise them into compliance, as was exposed by the leak in the minutes papers from the Government's SAGE team.

So, Instead, we had a much weaker Boris, and a weaker leader of the nation, can I say, "a much more deadlier variant of the old version of Boris whose own fear of something threatening him has caused him to be infected with the more deadlier "virus of fear" deadlier for the United Kingdom and its good and great people within. Something of far greater consequence and danger than a virus which threatens 0.03 percent of the population over 40 years old, i.e. three people in every thousand people who are over 40 years old, and threatens 0.02 % of the population among under 40s, i.e. two people every thousand people. So we are forced to face a downgraded version of the former Boris, a weaker variant but more deadly and who for some reason - I will explore later, he felt diminished enough or threatened or in a weakened state to be controlled by fear or greed or deception - deception from someone else or from his own self-deception or just pure fear from a Cabal of actors, a cabal of forces, or it could be that the new Boris was willing to turn-coat, willing to lie to his better judgement and better character, and willing to lie to the British people and deceive us all by taking advantage of a virus pandemic whose victims were predominantly over 80 where the average age of death is around 80 or 85. the World Economic Forum whose agenda he may have liked.

Anyway for some reason he chose to go against his former libertarian Boris and choose instead to choose the way of enslaving his own people and enslaving himself to choose to be the enslaver of Britain rather than the emancipator, to be instead the traitor of Britain and her people not their friend, But why? Whether it was because his wife, who is a Green agenda supporting Globalist herself pursued him, is anyone's guess although it could be an educated guess, if we were to find out that Boris new wife is the real reason he is told to proceed down the Globalists agenda of resetting the economy and following the way of the Banks, i.e. Banksters and Globalists

But why?

Whether it was because his wife, who is a Green-agenda activist, who seems to support the Globalists agenda, has pulled him into their agenda, is anyone's guess, although it could be an educated guess; certainly, before Boris' Covid-19 illness and before his relationship with Carrie Symonds, his libertine principles looked like they could have kept him away from such an extreme agenda of embracing their zero-net admission of carbon; or maybe, as I feel, he has always been an opportune politician and a man without a bone of principle throughout his body. This may be harsh of me to say, but I remember just before he proverbially "flung his hat in the ring" to be the leading voice after Nigel Farage in support of Brexit, Boris had written two different articles - one on the Remain argument and one on the Leave argument for the British Newspaper, "The Telegraph", when he said Britain's continued membership of the EU would be a "boon for the world and for Europe" in an unpublished newspaper column in which he wrestles with his decision to back or oppose Brexit.

Although Boris has since insisted the column was intended merely as a tool for his own thought process, calling it "semi-parodic", in that article, written days before a published version in which he backed leaving,

Johnson wrote of the EU: "This is a market on our doorstep, ready for further exploitation by British firms. The membership fee seems rather small for all that access. Why are we so determined to turn our back on it?"

We may one day find out that Boris' new wife, now Carrie Johnson, is the real reason Boris is told to proceed down the Globalists agenda of resetting the economy and following the way of the Banks, i.e. giving all the power to the leaders of the Banks, particularly, The Bank of England and Globalists in the same way that President Woodrow in the U.S. signed over the power of the Reserve to "the Banksters, i.e. the making and supply of the national currency to the Federal Reserve out of the hands of the people. Wilson negotiated the passage of the Federal Reserve Act, which created the Federal Reserve System and placed the power into a private Cabal just as what happened in the U.K. and the Bank of England. What is clear is the Federal Reserve and the Bank of

England has too much power, and that they may want to follow the example of China. What China is doing, or is about to do in the next year or so is to make their society completely cashless and rely instead on digital currency and digital bodily implanted information which Globalist organisations such the World Economic Forum headed by Klaus Schwab and Open Society Foundations headed by George Soros are planning, who have been waiting for years for a "good" crisis like the Coronavirus Virus "pandemic" to implement their evil Globalist plans.

So the real variants are the variants of fear, and lies that the Government tell us constantly in their fake computer data-models, and their fake data modelling designed to "put the fear of God into us to comply with their evil agenda. Boris is not at all optimistic - he may have been once, but not since this Covid-19 put the fear of high-hell into him he hasn't or someone or Cabal did, and since he has been held captive to fear so have the British people. It's not Boris' optimism, it's Boris 'pessimism which is the issue because he no longer has any optimism anymore while he keeps supporting prolonged lockdowns, and now that he looks like a terrified rabbit. He used to be very optimistic and robust and always upbeat, but not these days, he is completely different

But instead, the people of the U.K. got an entirely different Boris.

And so what became increasingly obvious is Boris looks threatened by someone or by some "Cabal" intent on moving him and the nation on an entirety different path, towards a Totalitarian State where none of us own anything or ourselves, where everyone is graded and given a credit-rating much the same as China, according to their compliance or noncompliance to the Government, i.e. "Big Brother reincarnated".

AND DEFINITELY DON'T BELIEVE A REPRESENTATIVE FROM THE GOVERNMENT WHO TURNS UP AT YOUR DOOR AND SAYS, "Hello, I'm from the Government, I'm here to help you." I didn't say that, I read it from the lips of Ronald Reagan, or I read his quotation.

Another way of saying that or a variant of his immortal words is, "Never trust anybody who knocks on your door and says, "Hi! I'm here from the Government and we are in the local area checking to see who hasn't had the vaccine yet, and who would like theirs."

From the very beginning, the Big Pharmaceutical companies were preparing to make a killing with their experimental vaccines, even though from the start of this pandemic, if the treatments for Covid-19 such as hydroxychloroquine and ivermectin had been rolled out with local doctors prescribing them, countless of thousands of peoples' lives would be saved.

For example, if you look at the case of India, a developing nation whose health care system is supposedly behind the first-world nation, the U.S.A., because they rolled out the Covid-19 treatments early only one hundred people in a million died of the disease there compared to 800 in a million in the U.S.A.

Of course, the BIG PHARMA greedy Cabal don't want the hydroxychloroquine treatment and other treatments, because they want to make their millions and peddle their vaccines, even though these vaccines have killed thousands.

When all this business about a mystery virus from China - actually, from the Chinese Communists Party -

first erupted onto our screens it was our Government Prime Minister, Boris Johnson who convened a Press Conference warning us about this new threat or this mystery virus. But what made our ears really prick up was his ominous words when he said, "I think by the end of this year, everyone will know someone who has died from this virus."

On the 23rd March, 2021, it was a full year to the day that Boris Johnson finally, after initially hesitating, ordered the entire U.K. to be shut down, to go into "lockdown" - that was ten days after in another news conference from Downing Street when he said with somber and seriousness in both his voice and face, "..And I must level with you, with the British public, that more families, many more families are going to lose loved ones before their time."

That was a full ten days before he finally ordered a full

lockdown on the 23rd March, 2020; that due to an airborne, mystery virus from China, which the Chinese Communist Government used their tactics of locking down entire Cities and towns to mitigate the infections, of which Italy followed suit in Milan and other cities and towns struck by Covid-19.

When I heard that I thought, "Boris knows something more than we do about how deadly this virus is, but he is not letting on."

But since then, we have learned a lot more about this virus, as well as a lot more about Boris Johnson and his inner character. We have learned that this virus called Covid-19 is not as deadly as Boris Johnson when he is controlled by a cabal of Globalists who are coercing him, or even threatening him to reset the economy and make it into a cashless society.

You may ask me, "How do I know that this country is being taken over, actually has already been taken over by some Cabal of Opportunists who are intent on forcing their agenda on us all?" And, "What is their agenda?"

My Answer: To end the circulation of physical money once and for all and instead introduce a digital currency which contains all the information the State knows about you. And without this new digital currency, no one will be able to buy or sell anything. To remove the high street banks once and for all who are mere middlemen.

So that's why I am convinced that this isn't about a virus which was either leaked from a lab, either purposely or as a bio-weapon which is wreaking havoc on us all, but it's really about the political establishment's response which is wreaking the real havoc on us, i.e. Boris under the threat for his safety or family's by a Cabal's of Globalists and banksters. You may call be a conspiracy theorist, but to me, these questions point to that scenario:

1. Why would Boris plunge the nation into three lockdowns when originally he was so reluctant to do so?

2. Why was Boris such a changed person from being always a self-proclaimed libertarian, and so upbeat and positive before his bout of Covid-19 to afterwards being so frightened looking, and always choosing the most restrictive and, under the threat of fear of death, tyrannical decision. For example, now that Boris and his Government have passed a law introducing the mandating of Covid-19 Status Passports for entry into the U.K. night-clubs, and which from the end of September, all those who work in the care industry will

be required to have been vaccinated, why was it that just a few years ago, Boris publicly said if anyone asked him for his National I.D. that he would crunch it into pieces and eat it.

If you observe what has been going on in the previous sixteen months, the real havoc hasn't been the virus so much as Boris and his underlings' response to this virus. And unfortunately, Boris is not the same man whom we elected to represent us - he is weak, and most alarming, he looks like he is beholden to that Cabal of opportunists who are forcing their own will and agenda onto us.

And if you feel that you are protected from such a Cabal since you live outside the U.K., that Cabal's agenda is worldwide for they are arch-Globalists. Whether it is the Great Reset being pushed by Klauss Schwab and his World Economic Forum – he is the

Founder - or whether they are beholden to a bigger and more evil enterprise, we don't know, or I don't know at this stage. But they're also saying or chanting the same mantra with both Boris Johnson and Joe Biden both saying the same Globalist mantra which is actually the Globalist's mantra of "Build Back Better". That's why I say, it's not about a virus, it's about resetting the economy. And those who are awake to this, know that this is much more than a pandemic - it's a "plandemic" - opportunists taking advantage of a good crisis. You may brand me as a conspiracy theorist, but, at least hear me out, as since this Covid-19 business started, there have been a few who were branded conspiracy theorists who were recently found to be telling the truth.

Yes, they want to relocate their assets. It's not so much the banks, it's the currencies and other asset holders who believe that the supply of money can be controlled in such a way that there is no need of money anymore, i.e. a cashless society. That's what the World Economic Forum want - they want to rescue you from your debt so that every possession is given to them and no one owns anything anymore. It's actually communism through the backdoor.

One day, maybe, soon, you will hear the Government or one of its agencies, maybe the Bank of England, after they stop printing money (during this pandemic, governments and banks have done nothing else but printing money - the lockdowns wasn't about a virus but about resetting the economy and bringing in a cashless society reliant on the State, after they realize printing money has produced hyper-inflation, they will announce the long awaited plan just like from the Chinese Communist Party, they will announce the end of all cash, and they will ask you to hand in your last notes of money, and instead receive another vaccine containing nano-technology with a digital chip containing all the information on you, when you go online, when you go out, even when you deficate or have sex.

But you better prepare for the time when all money loses its total value, i.e. make sure you have taken all your money out of the banks because legally they can seize all your money from inside their four walls, and bank vaults because that's what the new bail-in laws empowers them to do in the U.K. make sure you have bought stable currencies, or rather precious metals that keep their value, like gold, silver, etc.

The Three Instruments of the State
When the power of the State go to war, whether that war be a physical war or a culture war, they have four major instruments at their disposal:
1. Propaganda.

2. Fear, which Boris and his scientific advisors have made it into an art to "put the fear of God" into the populace.

3. Coercion by State Laws with threat of the army on the street, fines or imprisonment.

4. And the most severe are the threat of execution

You know that the State is using the first three instruments of their tyranny when they have have weoponized these against the good and great people of the United Kingdom, which Boris Johnson and his three main scientific advisors I have mentioned, ordered or used, and which his police forces and judges of the United Kingdom enforced .

When you see in the U.K., the Government is employing "mercenaries", they are paying over 260,000 to Director of a telephone App, when the

Government or Prime Minister stands in front while flanked with his chief scientific advisors who always give you data telling you that hundreds of thousands are going to die, or 1000's a day increase in infections unless we lockdown. Who days after going into lockdown, the public find out that the numbers the data and flow charts Boris and his advisors were using were skewed; as we have seen in the third lockdown easing, the day after we came out of lockdown completely, the case-numbers plummeted, which tells you something is fundamentally flawed about lockdowns.

The Lies and Skewed data from the Chief Scientist of the U.K.

YOU KNOW YOU ARE BEING LIED TO WHEN,

A GOVERNMENT REPRESENTATIVE TAKES A FEW MINUTES TO EXPLAIN THE REASON BEHIND WHY 60% OF THOSE ADMITTED TO HOSPITAL FOR COVID HAVE BEEN DOUBLE VACCINATED, AND THEN LATER HE TWEETS CORRECTING HIS STATEMENT HE MADE, THAT ITS NOT 60% OF COVID ADMISSIONS THAT ARE DOUBLE-VACCINATED BUT 60% OF UNVACCINATED.

HE COMPLETELY SWITCHED THE PERCENTAGE OF PEOPLE FROM DOUBLE VACCINATED TO UNVACCINATED.

WHY?

Because his correction serves his Government's agenda more, which is that the unvaccinated are causing all the new cases of hospitalisations and deaths, and they are the ones who are to blame.

You can Look at Patrick Vallance's Correction on You Tube. If like me, you take a closer look at Patrick's correction, it shows something is very, very smelly:

During Boris Johnson's Covid Press Announcements, Patrick Vallance, the U.K. Government's Chief Medical Advisor said,

"People in hospital who have been double-vaccinated, we know it's around 60 % of the people being admitted to hospital with covid have been double-vaccinated; and that's not surprising because the vaccines are not 100% effective - their very, very effective but not and a 100%, and as a higher proportion of the population is double-vaccinated, it's inevitable that those ten percent of that very large number remain at risk and therefore will be amongst the people who both catch the infection and end up in hospital."

"So whilst vaccines are very effective at reducing severe disease, they're also effective at reducing the chance of catching it and reducing the chance of passing it on, but they're slightly less effective of doing that than they are at preventing severe disease."

"And so, what we will see, as we get the.. let's say if everybody over the 18 had taken up the vaccine, then, of course, anybody who caught it would be double-vaccinated.

"So the answer is we should expect to see a higher proportion of people in hospital and catching the infection who are double-vaccinated, that is inevitable we should see because of the less than 100 % efficacy of the vaccines."

And then later, he tweeted the following tweet:

Correcting a statistic I gave at the press conference today, 19 July. About 60% of hospitalised from covid are not from double-vaccinated people, rather 60% of hospitalisations from Covid are currently from unvaccinated."

Can you see how utterly bizarre this is?
That he would spend. ..minutes explaining why there are around 60 % of hospitalisations are double-vaccinated, and then, later in the day change that to why about 60 % of those hospitalisations are unvaccinated.

Can you see why one Twitter user in response wrote the following Tweet?,

"An absolute bizarre "error" considering that you went on to explain exactly why the 60% figure was so high.

This is all very odd and suspicious."

This is a huge mistake you made, Mr. Pactrick Vallance, because it shows you were telling the truth in your first statement of 60 % of hospitalisations from double-vaccinated with your full explanation, but then, when you tried to correct your "truth" you exposed yourself as a lying.

Thus, the Government is dealing in lies and propaganda to serve their agenda to criminalise or target the unvaccinated in order to make them feel coerced into being vaccinated against their will. Just like when the Government minister, Michael Gove, went on national television and branded the unvaccinated as "selfish".

And the same is true on social media - it is the

unvaccinated who are being blamed for the new variant called Delta which is more infectious, and is targeting the young more. They say that the young are more vulnerable because they have not taken the vaccine as much as the older groups. They say that it is the unvaccinated that are driving these new cases and variants.

And if propaganda doesn't do the trick, the next tool the State has or had up their sleeve is fear, then if fear doesn't work, then they will, and have amended their laws and reverted to the threat of fines or imprisonment; just like when the U.K. Government said you need two vaccines to be immune from Covid, and then later, they told you that those two vaccines effectiveness dwindled, and so you need regular boosters, even though, now, in hindsight we learn that recent studies show that your natural immunity is far more effective, and that those vaccines actually increased your viral load of Covid in your body or immune system, and actually are, in fact, the driving force of the variant Delta. According to the propaganda, these variants such as the Delta virus are being driven by the unvaccinated, but if you speak with the honest epidemiologists, they will tell you that if you have a vaccine that is not killing off a virus but only reducing its efficacy, then if you are a virus and you feel your effect is weakened or that you face annihilation, what you do is you mutate, or in the case of the Covid-19 virus, you produce a variant form of Covid-19, thus it is not the unvaccinated which are driving these more deadly variants but the vaccinated.

If we go on like this or if the Boris Government continues along these lines, then they would be an administration which manufacturers lies at the rate of a lying machine in order to keep the British public in a continued state of fear, as this is one of the State instruments as well as propaganda. And maybe, Boris will invite bidders to tend their designs to build himself and his chief scientists the first ever lying machine with a Government patent. A lying machine with the slogan on the side, "WE ARE FOLLOWING THE SCIENCE!"

The Care Home Crisis Dereliction of Duty.
At the beginning of the crisis, 46,000 elderly were told to leave hospitals to make room for covid cases without being tested, that in April, 2020, nine days after ordering the first lockdown, the director effectively wrote the death warrant for 8,000 odd elderly patients to be sent into care homes without being tested.

And now from the end of September, all hospital and care workers have to be double vaccinated, otherwise they can't work in the care industry.

Throughout this Covid-crisis, Boris, always insisted that his priority was to save the N.H.S., yet, how many lives were sacrificed on his alter of the N.H.S? When the N.H.S. was founded by Lord Aneurin Bevan of the Labour Party, it's was set up to care and look after the good and great people of the United Kingdom without charge, but Boris has completely switched that to, asking the people of the United Kingdom to look after the N.H.S.

Now, after such a short-sighted policy, the N.H.S. has never had so many sick people waiting to be treated, and how many millions of patients died early because they were not given timely treatment or tests, or because all cancer, stroke, heart and other patients were banned, or feared going near a hospital because of Covid-19, and because the Government reserved hospital beds for only Covid patients.

And, also, sadly, as we observed from "over the Pond" in New York, how hospital ships sent into New York harbour for emergencies, were not used because of political decisions rather than patients care - I mean the new hospitals built by the British good and brave soldiers - the Nightingale hospitals named after our leading nurse, Florence Nightingale - were largely left empty throughout their availability because this "Covid-crisis" just didn't become overwhelming for the N.H.S. on the whole.

I don't know if you have read the book by George Orwell called 1984. He introduces us to new concepts or words which will be prevalent in the Dystopian world. One of those words is "truth" issued by the "Ministry of Truth" which is, in reality, far from the truth and should be rather called "The Ministry of Lies", but in the world of 1984, truth is lies and lies is truth.

Fear is the most debilitating emotion known to man because so many millions of people, as we have learned from history, can so easily come under the spell of fear, when they feel threatened.

And now we have BIG BROTHER in the form of the British National Health Service App, which has, the last month or so been wreaking havoc across the country with their pandemic, causing up to half of the workforce to be "pinged" on their phones, resulting in staff-shortages across the nation, as well as food-shortages on shelves in some areas;and last week, that N.H.S.App was "upgraded" by the Government technicians so that all existing users of the Tract and Trace App could upgrade it, or it automatically upgraded with the Covid-status Passport. SURPRISE, SURPRISE!

Now we learn that the N.H.S. is as pressured, now at the height of Summer, as in January -but not because of the Covid-19 surbe but rather because people are being "pinged" by the N.H.S. App, and the Test and Trace Department.

One British man said he originally thought that it would take a few months to turn the U.K. into a digital reliant or I.D. certificate card reliant but in three days it has almost occurred. Last Monday, the Government snuck through - actually rushed through legislation that demands that by the end of September, all nightclubs will have to show a Covid, proof of double vaccination on your smart-phone. Now does that concern or worry you? It concerns me.

Boris Johnson, the U.K.'s PM, has already announced that from October all care workers should be double vaccinated. From October, if the legislation is approved by parliament, staff and volunteers working in care homes registered by the Care Quality Commission (CQC) will have to have two doses of a covid-19 vaccine unless they have a medical exemption. This applies to England, only.

The requirement will apply to full or part time agency staff, workers employed directly by the care home or provider, and volunteers working with residents. Those coming into a care home to do other work, such as healthcare workers and CQC inspectors, will also have to follow the new rules.

The Government has announced that from the end of September, all N.H.S. staff, including all those who work in the public care industry – cleaners etc, and even those who visit any care homes have to be doubled vaccinated. Also, Boris has also announced that from the end of September, for all large gatherings and venues holding at least 2000, as well as nightclubs, even churches and pubs, and restaurants, all visitors will have to produce a Covid-vaccination status passport on their phones.

In the U.K., vaccination against people's will, has not been tried since the Vaccination Act of 1853, and at that time, there was such a BACKLASH, the law was overturned and the phrase "Conscientious Objector" sprung from the PUSHBACK:

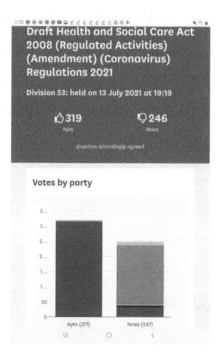

AND NOW, THE GOVERNMENT ARE PREPARING PROGRAMS FOR TEENAGERS TO BE VACCINATED BY THESE VACCINES,
and most alarming are the reasons why children are being vaccinated:

1.To ensure that we reach an almost full vaccination of the population; in other words, they are using the children to protect the adults, which is actually against international law.

2. To ensure that children do not catch the Covid-19 virus, however, the truth is, vaccination among children is not necessary because children predominantly have a strong enough immune system, unless their immune system is compromised.

THIS IS THE CLASSICAL CASE OF THE CURE IS WORSE THAN THE DISEASE!

I'm afraid to say the people living in the U.K. have become ensnared to fear because they let themselves be led by their leaders who are controlled by fear.

Now That Covid-19 Vaccination Certificates are being Introduced in the U.K, Where are we Heading?

Despite Boris Johnson saying only two weeks ago about terminus day or freedom day, or if not now when, he has U-Turned by capitulating to the fear-mongers or fear seduced among his advisors in SAGE team or NERVETAG team, or fellow ministers or anyone else controlling him and thus controlling the entire U.K. of 66.65 million to a certain extent. Now his government just passed an amendment to a 2008 law which will force all care workers to be vaccinated.

We are not that far behind this state of affairs in England, where care home workers face mandatory vaccination and large indoor venues have been urged to require vaccine passports.

I used to think that the U.K. was edging ever closer, i.e. CREEPINGLY to a dystopian 1984 existence, but now with the sudden introduction of Covid-19 vaccination status passports at the end of September is a slippery slide into the abyss of a dystopian BIG BROTHER WATCHING.

As I'm writing this, last night in the U.K. House of Commons where politicians meet to make new laws, a new law was passed by the Conservative Party Government of Boris Johnson's Government to mandate all care workers to have the vaccine, meaning to force all care workers to get a Covid-19 vaccine. Some care workers will go along with it, some will not. The result of this I believe will be that an awful lot of good care workers will leave the profession of which the care industry cannot afford to lose, because most of them will probably be replaced with a lesser quality of worker, definitely if a less experienced person is employed, instead. It was these precious workers who were risking their lives last year when the pandemic was raging through our hospitals, when there was such a shortage of personal protection equipment, including masks.

The law is actually an amendment from a 2008 Law which has been changed to attach some Covid-19 laws but what these laws says are exceedingly ominous and are taking this country and all of us down a very dark road i.e. forced coercive vaccinations among its citizens, the first with now Boris contemplating as well as Emanuel Macron contemplating mandating forced vaccines for the entire population p, in other words, otherwise having a two-tier system or actually having a two-tier system whereby there would effectively be a two system citizen much similar to North Korea whereby you would be discriminated against if you haven't been vaccinated.

Here in the U.K., the possibility of mass Covid-19 Immunity Passports for everybody mandated by the government is now a very real possibility after on the 13th July a law was passed, actually an existing law which was upgraded to introduce mandated vaccinations for all care workers in the N.H.S. and other national care organisations. It came at the same time as France or the French Government and the U.K, Government both mandating that all healthcare workers have to be vaccinated has entered a dark, ominous chapter.

If you think that the Government did that for your health, then think again. Nowadays, the Government N.H.S. track and trace App is out of control and is putting the nation and its people on a road to food shortages.

If you think that such a law seems harmless, well think

again, in my opinion, it is the very beginning of a process of the Government infiltrating your own body (i.e. Internet of Bodies) and inserting numerous sensors which can track everything you say, everything you do, your activity online so with that wealth of information on you, they can categorize you as whether you are a Compliant or a Non-Compliant just as North Korea and China are doing. They can even place tiny nano-DNA viruses or RNA virus-making factories into your bloodstream just like these new mRNA-Vaccines - but it's all done in the name of your health.

Examples of Internet of Bodies (IoB) Technologies propagated by the World Economic Forum

But if you want to see how the Internet of Bodies fits into a great reset, like the one the World Economic Forum is touting, look no further than China's social credit system that "uses enormous amounts of aggregated data, including health records, on individuals to determine their trustworthiness and to incentivize desired behaviors," according to the RAND article.

A population that knows it is being watched will change its behavior to conform to the norms, and its citizens will police themselves.

Thus, the Internet of Bodies is a tool that can serve multiple purposes — it can revolutionize healthcare for the benefit of all; it can be used to monitor, track, and prevent global crises before they manifest, and it can be turned into an apparatus for manipulating human behaviour in order to achieve the desired outcomes of the global elite.

Contact tracing is also a tool for complete social control, keeping tabs on a nation's so-called deplorable or undesirable citizens.

Think social justice policing via contact tracing — not just through mobile phones, but tracking chips implanted in the human body.

Today, the World Economic Forum is fully behind the use of the Internet of Bodies, and actively supports digital health passports, i.e. Covid Passports and contract tracing apps, i.e. the Pre-Covid Passport.

If you think that the idea behind contact tracing apps is just for tracking people infected by viruses, think again.

The same technology was used by the CCP [Chinese Communist Party] to develop an app that literally alerts citizens with a warning when they come within 500 meters of someone who is in debt, according to the WEF "Global Risks Report 2019."

"The app has created what's essentially a map of 'deadbeat debtors,' according to Chinese state media, and shows you the debtor's exact location, though it's unclear if the displayed information includes a name or photo."

So, while the World Economic Forum urges greater Internet of Bodies use and contact tracing, the technology is not just for tracking the spread of a virus.

Contact tracing is also a tool for complete social control that keeps tabs on a nation's so-called deplorable or undesirable citizens.
Think social justice policing via contact tracing — not

just through mobile phones, but tracking chips implanted in the human body.

"Widespread Internet of Bodies use might increase the risk of physical harm, espionage, and exploitation of data by adversaries" — RAND Corporation report on Internet of Bodies Risks, RAND Corporation.

The RAND report also warned that "widespread Internet of Bodies use might increase the risk of physical harm, espionage, and exploitation of data by adversaries."

Indeed, if state-sponsored hackers or criminal organizations were to gain access to a medical device used by a high-profile target, the hackers could simply switch it off and assassinate their target.

On top of the geopolitical risks, the RAND report warned that the Internet of Bodies could also "increase health outcome disparities, where only people with financial means have access to any of these benefits."

However, this seems an unlikely scenario because the WEF doesn't like to see one nation gain too much power. It prefers balance. It wants every country to follow the rules. It wants a technocratic Utopia.

"Authoritarianism is easier in a world of total visibility and traceability, while democracy may turn out to be more difficult" — World Economic Forum report

As such, the World Economic Forum would like to see the Internet of Bodies regulated uniformly across the globe, and the Davos elite routinely call for its ethical governance, but that doesn't mean the surveillance would go away.

Not at all.

It just means that everybody would be spied on equally after having consented to the Draconian measures dressed-up as serving the greater good.

At its heart, the Internet of Bodies is dependent upon collecting tons of biometric data, which will "allow new forms of social control," according to the World Economic Forum Global Risks 2019 report.

The World Economic Forum concluded two years ago that "authoritarianism is easier in a world of total visibility and traceability, while democracy may turn out to be more difficult."

Now, the World Economic Forum wants to exploit the Fourth Industrial Revolution under the great reset agenda, and it has massive support from the media, world leaders, and captains of industry alike.

Klaus Schwab, the founder and director of the World Economic Forum, had already called for the great reset back in 2014, but decided in June, 2020, that this was the year to enact the scheme because the coronavirus crisis had presented a "rare but narrow window of opportunity."

And in order to make the Davos elites' globalist Utopia a reality, universal trust in the increasingly invasive uses of emerging technologies will be required.

If you are willing to believe that a global, un-elected body of bureaucrats based in Switzerland, i.e. World Economic Forum has your best interest at heart, then you are willing to accept that your corporeal autonomy, physical privacy, and mental freedom may be compromised to serve the greater good.

Fears have been fuelled by the fact that the £250,000 contract to provide the cloud software for the certification system was handed to Entrust, an American IT firm previously involved in rolling out national ID systems in Albania, Ghana and Malaysia. Tory civil rights campaigner and former cabinet minister David Davis told The Telegraph Covid passports were "a very bad idea", "intrusive" and "completely out of the tradition of Britain". Pointing out there were 9,000 data leaks last year from government records, he said: "There are very serious civil liberties issues, serious issues of practicality and serious issues of discrimination." A government spokesperson said: "

The NHS Covid pass allows an individual to demonstrate Covid status. It is not a form of national ID

card and it never will be. The Covid Status Certification review, published last week, concluded that there was a public health benefit to using the NHS Covid pass."
A poll by Savanta ComRes released last night showed a third of adults aged 18-34 had deleted the NHS Covid-19 app, with more intending to remove it after "Freedom Day" on July 19.

If you think that such technology is years away from us in the distant future, then think again.

CHAPTER TWO.

Why Weren't the Public Informed of the Treatments Available as well as the Preventions for Covid-19?

Now that the Big Pharmaceutical companies have rolled out their various vaccines, why are the British public not fully given the information about the real effectiveness of treatments against Covid-19, both as a preventive treatment and as a possible cure? For example, there is mounting evidence for the effectiveness of treatments such as the following:

Vitamin D, i.e. natural from limited exposure to the Sun, as well as vitamin D supplements. Hydroxychloroquine which has been used for over forty years against malaria, yet, there is growing evidence of its effectiveness against Covid-19, as both a preventative and a treatment. Actually, since President

Trump advocated its use, it became something of a political football when Trump's enemies demonized the drug, after demonizing him. As we have seen, once Trump favours something, that something falls out of favour with his enemies for one reason, alone. HATRED FOR TRUMP.

So, let me now reference a good, more balanced source which catalogues the various treatments for Covid-19 from Harvard Health Publishing from Harvard Medical School: Link:

The Possible Treatments For Covid-19 Recommended by the U.S. Government for Early Covid-19

Just to Reference One of the Treatments Recommended by the U.S. Government for Early Covid-19
In November 2020, the FDA granted emergency use

authorization to two monoclonal antibody treatments (bamlanivimab, made by Eli Lilly; and a combination of casirivimab and imdevimab, made by Regeneron). Both treatments have been approved for non-hospitalized adults and children over age 12 with mild to moderate COVID-19 symptoms who are at risk for developing severe COVID-19 or being hospitalized for it. In these patients, the approved treatments can reduce the risk of hospitalization and emergency room visits. These therapies must be given intravenously (by IV) soon after developing symptoms.

For further advice, the best way is to consult your doctor.

Why have Governments around the world not fully investigated these treatments and others, more natural treatment as well as prevention; for example, the hormone vitamin D as the most effective treatment apart from your own Natural Immunity?

I learned something which, if the public were told the effectiveness of limited exposure to Sun or the taking of vitamin-D supplements as a treatment and preventive for Covid-19 instead of issuing face-mask mandates, this could have saved thousands of lives. That vitamin-D is a vital ingredient to the entire approach to this Covid-19 virus including any of its mutations:

Why is Vitamin D so Effective in the Fight Against Covid-19?

Not a lot of people know this but vitamin D is not just a vitamin but is actually a hormone. To be given that name hormone is actually very important because only a hormone has the authority to enter the human cell and its software, the DNA and alter its codes of genetic material. In other words, hormone is a agent of the cell who has the authority to actually penetrate even through- by its own receptors being soluble which means it has the power to penetrate the cell wall; you can envision the cell as another world because the cell is of course protected from the outside and is a complete bubble and that vitamin-D can actually enter the DNA and can actually change the content of that DNA, and therefore, top mutation or stop the RNA from mutating.

But where did I get this amazing Vitamin D?
One is absolutely free while the other will cost you.

And there are two sources for this Vitamin D.

1. The Sun - which is completely natural
2. Buying vitamin supplements which is not free.

And these scientists tell us that vitamin-D protects us and treats Covid-19 better than anything. The Vitamin D derived from sunlight.

So in other words, vitamin-D is a real game-changer in the fight against Covid-19

But why aren't our Government and their advisors telling us this or at least discussing the importance and encouraging its citizens to expose themselves daily to at least twenty minutes of sunlight.

An Indonesian study found that among a group of all Covid-19 patients who all had Covid-19 disease and showing symptoms, they found ninety-nine percent had vitamin D deficiency. Yet, the U.K. Government banned the U.K. population from sunbathing in public parks and beaches during 2020. And when in the first two weekends after the first Lockdown when the British people flocked to the beaches for respite and sunbathing the Health Secretary said that he was shocked that so many people are breaking the rules.

It looks very likely because these vaccine companies want to enjoy the profits of their vaccines and have long ago placed their profit margins incentives before the actual welfare of those suffering.

See, I hope what you and I have learned over the past two years through being subjected to more pain and suffering at the hands of an increasingly compromised Prime Minister rather than at the hands of a virus should open up our eyes to the way, actually the Globalists have been waiting for years for their opportunity to bring in what is called, "The Great Reset" (which isn't actually great) now before you close my book and dismiss me as just a conspiracy theory nut-job, please hear me out by first reading what I have to say.

The U.K. has really Been Through The Rack - Three Times

We who are living, here, in the U.K. have really been put through the rack these past twelve months by the Boris Johnson Government; actually, three racks or three "lockdowns" as they are called, when the Government and Boris Johnson and his two scientists who flack him on his left and right, who always give the worst-case scenario, who, maybe they do that to cover their backs in case this disease of Covid-19 did actually sweep through the population and kill millions as they seem to envision it would - but if we look at past government and civilizations we never quarantined the healthy to protect the hospital service but always quarantined the sick to protect the healthy; we never quarantined the healthy to protect the sick but quarantined the sick to protect the healthy; we never closed whole nations until the Chinese Communist Party did.

There was a book called Black Mirror which is a

modern dystopian story of 1984 updated, of which, according to the imdb website,

Dystopian imaginings are no longer just the preserve of literature. Recent award-winning films such as Ex Machina (2015) and Her (2013) render vivid speculative worlds in which our inner life is exposed by technology. But one of the most pertinent excavations of the social consequences of contemporary technology appeared on the small screen, not in cinemas: Charlie Brooker's Black Mirror.

The first episode of the most recent series in particular echoes Shteyngart's parable of a world in which we are all reduced to a constantly fluctuating metric – friends, colleagues and strangers rate each social interaction. This metric is then used to sort us into categories and grant or deny us access to goods, services and public spaces. Think the idea of an aggregate "social credit" score is fantasy? China's proposed Sesame Credit scheme, whereby every citizen will be awarded a "social credit" score, suggests that science fiction increasingly resembles documentary.

CHAPTER THREE.

MY ATTEMPTED ESCAPE FROM BIG BROTHER.

The next day I was awakened to the sound of a voice command coming from my phone, the voice said,

"A very good morning to you, Ladies and Gentlemen, We have a very important announcement from your benevolent Government. Today, is a very special day, because we have a very exciting announcement to make:

"Your Government, Her Majesty's Government invites every subject of the realm a once in a life-time opportunity. If you have any debt which you would like to dispose of, if you have been saddled with a debt which has been weighing on you like a heavy millstone around your neck, and if you really want to get rid of that debt, then we invite you to let the Government of

Her Benevolent Majesty, your benevolent Government take that debt from you, know matter how big or small; THAT'S RIGHT, LADIES AND GENTLEMEN, YOU HEARD IT RIGHT, WE WILL TAKE ALL YOUR DEBT FROM YOU, and in exchange all we ask is that you make yourself more available to Her Majesty's Government. Yes, Ladies and Gentlemen, you have heard that right. "We are offering you the opportunity to get rid of all your debt once and for all; and that's why we are calling this day, JUBILEE DAY, for just like the Jewish people in the Bible, every fifty years they had the year of JUBILEE when they cancelled all their debts and when all land was reverted to the nation state and allowed assets were cancelled; The biblical requirement is that the Jubilee year was to be treated like a Sabbatical year, with the land lying fallow, but also required the compulsory return of all property to its original owners.."

Well, we are doing much better, we are offering you

this opportunity of a lifetime, any day and everyday for perpetuity when everyone will be offered the amazing opportunity to completely clear them."

Such an offer from the Government many will find difficulty to resist with the promise of freeing themselves of all the stress of their unwanted debt.

But what are in those injections?

They are tiny, nano, mRNA chips containing at the sub-microscopic scale little digital chips with Q codes on them containing all your digital information containing all the information on you, as well as the ability to hook you and your memory to the Internet of bodies to trace not only your past but also your present, in order for the State to predict your future decisions, to see whether you are a State Compliant or State Rogue, or somewhere in between, just like China or North Korea categorize you into one of three boxes, compliant, non-compliant or wavering.

I found out later that many actually millions had taken up the Government's offer of clearing all their debts or of owning their debt or underwriting their debt.

Would you?

The Government are gradually taking away your freedoms and rights in the name of your health

Just as in the U.S. the Biden administration and Joe Biden are shutting down Americans free speech or 2nd Amendment in the name of, saving lives because they say these vaccine Articles on the dangers of vaccines are misinformation and so they need to be shut down for saving lives.

If you've read the Dystopian novel 1984 everything the regime does is excused as for protecting the State, the same is true of North Korea. If you think it's just about your health or the public's health, think again.

Last night, in the U.K's House of Commons this legislation was passed.

If you think that the N.H.S. test and trace and the N.H.S App was only about your health and wellbeing, THINK AGAIN because it is one step towards what the people who are taking advantage of this international pandemic - actually they have been waiting for years for their opportunity to pounce. These Globalists want to have a system where every citizen is hooked up to what they have been dreaming of is called an "Internet of bodies", the next step after their Internet of Things, listen to this quote from Klauss Schwab, the Founder of World Economic Forum, who said, after establishing the Internet of Things. from the World Economic Forum in Davos, they want to bring into reality, and are planning a system of everybody being hooked up to the internet with a centralised controlled by billionaires, bankers etc, whereby everyone swallows into their body a pill which contains numerous sensors that track everything you say, everything you do, and you feel.

You can call this creeping Dystopian 1984 existence for us all which it what it is because its one step closer to all of us being hooked up to what's called a "Internet of Bodies" which is actually in the pipe line of certain organisations and individuals - (technocrats or tachnointiativers, stakeholders rather than mere stockholders) Globalist leaders who they are actually planning the "Internet of bodies" whereby every citizen and person in the planet has swallowed numerous censors which are hackable bio-health sensors which can relay to the internet everything about you including when you have sex, when you defecate, when you go out, when you are online and what online sites you have logged onto, where you roam when you go out, even what words you speak and what emotions pass through you. Such a Internet of Bodies will give Governments unprecedented access so that every person will be given an i.e. code which identifies you and categorizes you as being a coercive, a semi-coercive or a non-coercive, i.e. a rogue element, enemy of the state, who needs to be controlled by forced coercion and punishment, whereby semi-rogues will have their liberties curtailed or even they will be incarcerated just like happens everyday in North Korea; even threatened with all liberties, much in the same way as North Korea as such a system of categorizing everyone of its million into three different tiers, much in the same way as China is doing now with its undesirable elements of the State, i.e. the Uguhian people who it has even an app which alerts others if you venture within a 100 meters of these people.

CHAPTER FOUR.

More Power into the Hands of Less and Less People.

Archibald "Darkforces Takeover" Turncoat was originally a democrat, in the British sense of the word, someone who followed political advancement through the rule of law and democratically elected means.

But later, after enjoying a taste of power, and enjoying the sweet trappings of power he started to get designs far beyond his station, and way beyond the constraints of the ballot box and law.

Isn't that what happens to all those individuals who begin to become corrupted or who let themselves be influenced by dark forces, and Archibald was a man who was on a downward spiral into the abyss of ever corrupting forces of darkness who saw in him a willing collaborator? A willing and compromised soul who was ready to sell his soul to the Devil in exchange for his own pay-off or dividends- he had long ago weighed up the benefits and loss of exchanging any morals and conscience he once had.

Certainly since he had first moved into Silicon Valley and set up his own social media platform to rival the likes of Facebook, as an alternative to Facebook which he branded as a kinder, more honest face alternative to Facebook Incorporated, also setting up an alternative search engine to Google whose business plan was to somehow rival Amazon who had gone one step further than the Google search engine because it was a search Engine with a checkout at the end.

Like Facebook, not so much Google it had sold-out its integrity for greed in trading-in its users privacy for dollars; in other words, going against its stated Terms of Conditions, it had sold its users information to a third party for financial benefit.

C.S. Lewis had something to say about the power of Big Tech, although they weren't around in his day, he could envision their spectre approaching. What did C.S. Lewis write as a warning about the power of too much power in the hands of too few in control of our ever diminishing rights or free speech and free domain content?

To lose freedom of thought (FT) is to lose our dignity, our democracy and our very selves. Accordingly, the right to Freedom of Thought receives absolute protection under international human rights law. To lose sovereignty over our minds is to lose our dignity, our democracy, and even our very selves. Such sovereignty is termed mental autonomy. This is "the specific ability to control one's own mental functions," which include attention, memory, planning, rational thought and decision making (Metzinger, 2013). Dignity, "the presumption that one is a person whose actions, thoughts and concerns are worthy of intrinsic respect, because they have been chosen, organized and guided" (Nuffield Council on Bioethics, 2002, p. 121, italics added) requires mental autonomy. Democracies, in which citizens choose the laws that bind them (Johnson and Cureton, 2019), are only possible if citizens are mentally autonomous. The ability to think freely is so essential to our identity that to violate it is to deprive us "of personhood altogether" (Halliburton, 2009, p. 868).

Law must hence safeguard mental autonomy. International human rights law does this through the right to freedom of thought (FoT) (Nowak, 1993). In the United States, Freedom of Thought is protected by the

Bill of Rights (Blitz, 2010; Richards, 2015). Given the centrality of the right to Freedom of Thought to both personhood and democracy, one may expect it to be clearly defined and frequently exercised. One would be wrong in both cases.

The right to Freedom of Thought is poorly defined. Attempts to sketch its contours have been negligible (Kolber, 2016). It is unclear what counts as thought, what qualifies as a violation of the right, whether the right should be absolute and, if not, what would justify its violation (Mendlow, 2018).

"If we find ourselves with a desire that nothing in this world can satisfy, the most probable explanation is that we were made for another world."
C.S. Lewis
And these days, I certainly feel that all these fast encroaching dark forces taking away all our traditional freedoms and rights which only sixteen months ago we

thought they were non-negotiable rights, are taking our nation and this world down a very darks path, that I believe only a saviour like Jesus Christ can rescue us all from. Only back in March 2020, we thought all these freedoms were freedoms that thousand of patriots before us had died for, and that no one would ever take from us or future generations again.

Our rights and freedoms, we obviously took them for granted as much as the air we breathe, as Margaret Thatcher called them, "indivisible" rights and freedoms.

But now we know, if we don't protest or pray to Jesus Christ to save us, they will even try to take away the right to breathe clean and safe air, in the name of our health, just like they have tried to take away all our other rights in the name of our health. Rights such as the right to protest using non-violence, i.e. the right to assemble peacefully and protest our grievances against the State which Boris Johnson's Government and his policemen and judges have taken away, the right to go out when we want, the right to gather for freedom of religion, the right to consent to our own choices regarding what we allow to go into our bodies and medical treatment etc.

After feeling thoroughly abused and violated by all these shenanigans over the previous sixteen months, I decided I wanted to take a holiday with my grandmother, Ethel Bloggs, who the Government had banned me from hugging for almost a year.

CPSIA information can be obtained
at www.ICGtesting.com
Printed in the USA
BVHW011013070921
616156BV00021B/144